# So Much to Do

## William Chin
## Illustrated by Doreen Gay-Kassel

"Father," asked Jen,
"what is Yun doing?"

"Yun is coming with me.
We have to do everything
on this list,"
said Father.

1. Bookstore
2. Post Office
3. Food Store
4. ?

2

"Can I come, too?" asked Jen.

"Yes," said Father.
"We have so much to do."

First they went to the bookstore.

"We have to get the new book
that Grandfather wants," said Father.

"Father, what's the last thing on the list?" asked Yun.

"Will it be fun?" asked Jen.

"You'll see," said Father.

At the post office, they stood
in a very long line.

"We're picking up a package
for your grandfather.
His brother sent him a few gifts
from China," said Father.

"I don't like all this waiting,"
said Jen.

Next they went to the food store.

"This is taking so long," said Jen.

"Why do we need all these things?"
asked Yun.

"We're making a special dinner
tonight," said Father.

The girls were tired of waiting and standing in line.
They wanted to do something fun.

"When will we do something fun?"
asked Jen.

"We will soon," said Father.

11

12

"Do you know where we are now?" asked Father.

"I do!" said Yun.

"I know where we are, too!" said Jen.
"This is Grandfather's bakery."

The girls ran to open the door.

"Hi, children," said Grandfather.
"Have you been busy today?"

"Oh yes," said Jen.
"We've had so much to do."

14

"Now I know why we did
so many things," said Yun.
"We did them all for you,
Grandfather."

"Happy birthday," the girls said, smiling at Grandfather.